W9-CTR-729

exton, Colleen A., 1967-
ust
WITHDRAWN
201
3305222674511
h

# EXPLORING COUNTRIES

# Australia

by Colleen Sexton

BLASTOFF!
5
READERS

BELLWETHER MEDIA · MINNEAPOLIS, MN

Note to Librarians, Teachers, and Parents:

**Blastoff! Readers** are carefully developed by literacy experts and combine standards-based content with developmentally appropriate text.

**Level 1** provides the most support through repetition of high-frequency words, light text, predictable sentence patterns, and strong visual support.

**Level 2** offers early readers a bit more challenge through varied simple sentences, increased text load, and less repetition of high-frequency words.

**Level 3** advances early-fluent readers toward fluency through increased text and concept load, less reliance on visuals, longer sentences, and more literary language.

**Level 4** builds reading stamina by providing more text per page, increased use of punctuation, greater variation in sentence patterns, and increasingly challenging vocabulary.

**Level 5** encourages children to move from "learning to read" to "reading to learn" by providing even more text, varied writing styles, and less familiar topics.

Whichever book is right for your reader, Blastoff! Readers are the perfect books to build confidence and encourage a love of reading that will last a lifetime!

This edition first published in 2011 by Bellwether Media, Inc.

No part of this publication may be reproduced in whole or in part without written permission of the publisher. For information regarding permission, write to Bellwether Media, Inc., Attention: Permissions Department, 5357 Penn Avenue South, Minneapolis, MN 55419.

Library of Congress Cataloging-in-Publication Data

Sexton, Colleen A., 1967-
Australia / by Colleen Sexton.
   p. cm. – (Blastoff! readers: Exploring countries)
Summary: "Developed by literacy experts for students in grades three through seven, this book introduces young readers to the geography and culture of Australia"–Provided by publisher.
Includes bibliographical references and index.
ISBN 978-1-60014-473-8 (hardcover : alk. paper)
1. Australia–Juvenile literature. I. Title.
DU96.S44 2010
994–dc22                                  2010006450

Text copyright © 2011 by Bellwether Media, Inc. BLASTOFF! READERS and associated logos are trademarks and/or registered trademarks of Bellwether Media, Inc.

Printed in the United States of America, North Mankato, MN.

080110     1162

# Contents

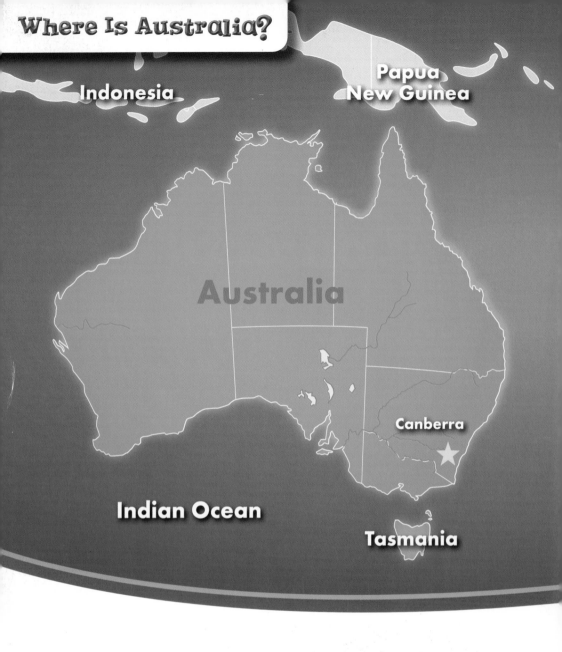

Indonesia

Papua New Guinea

Australia

Canberra

Indian Ocean

Tasmania

Australia's nickname is the "Land Down Under" because it lies below the **equator** in the southern half of the world. Australia is the only country that covers a whole **continent**! With an area of 2,988,902 square miles (7,741,220 square kilometers), it is the sixth-largest country in the world.

**Pacific Ocean**

**Did you know?**
Australia lies about 7,000 miles (11,265 kilometers) southwest of the United States. An airplane trip from California to Australia takes more than 14 hours!

**New Zealand**

Water surrounds Australia. The country sits between the Indian Ocean and the Pacific Ocean. Australia's nearest neighbors are New Zealand to the southeast, and Indonesia and Papua New Guinea to the north. The nearby island of Tasmania is part of Australia. Canberra is Australia's capital city.

Did you know?

Seasons in countries south of the equator are the opposite of seasons north of the equator. When it is winter in the United States, it is summer in Australia!

Most of Australia's cities are on the country's eastern edge. The weather is mild there. Sandy beaches and rocky cliffs line the eastern shore. The coastline gives way to hills that are green with forests and crops. Farther inland, low mountains stretch north to south. To the west, most of Australia is dry, flat land where few people live. Australians call this huge region the **Outback**. Here, sheep roam the grassy **plateaus**. Giant sand **dunes** spread across deserts. Some of the hottest weather on Earth is in the Outback.

## fun fact

A giant rock called Ayers Rock, or *Uluru*, rises from the sand dunes of the Outback. It measures 1.5 miles (2.4 kilometers) long and 1,100 feet (335 meters) high.

The Great Barrier Reef stretches
1,400 miles (2,250 kilometers)
along Australia's northeastern coast.
Colorful **corals** have built the reef over
thousands of years. These tiny, soft animals
build hard skeletons around their bodies.
The skeletons stay behind when the corals die.
New corals live on top of the skeletons. The Great
Barrier Reef is like a city under the sea. About 1,500
kinds of fish find shelter there. Dolphins, sea turtles,
and whales swim nearby. Sponges, sea stars, snails,
and thousands of other small animals
also live on the reef.

! **fun fact**

The Great Barrier Reef is the only living thing on Earth that can be seen from space!

**Did you know?**

The world's largest group of dugongs lives around the Great Barrier Reef. These large, gray mammals are also known as sea cows. They graze on sea grasses like cows graze on grass.

dugong

koala

Australia is known for its unusual creatures. Platypuses swim in the country's streams. They have webbed feet, fur, and bills like ducks. Nearly 700 kinds of birds live in Australia. The kookaburra is one such bird. Its call sounds like a person laughing. Emus are large birds that cannot fly. They run everywhere.

kookaburra

emu

kangaroo

**fun fact**
Red kangaroos can hop on their hind legs up to 40 miles (64 kilometers) per hour. They can jump a distance of 30 feet (9 meters) in one hop!

Wild dogs called dingoes roam throughout much of the country. They hunt and howl at night. Kangaroos, Tasmanian devils, and wombats are **marsupials** found in Australia. They carry their young in pouches attached to their bellies. Koalas are marsupials too. They eat only the leaves of **eucalyptus** trees and rarely drink water.

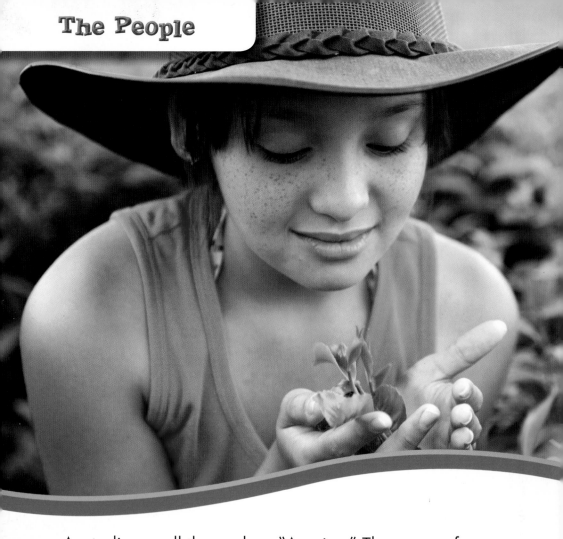

Australians call themselves "Aussies." They come from many backgrounds. Most of the country's 21 million people have **ancestors** from Great Britain or Ireland. In the mid-1900s, **immigrants** began to arrive from other countries. They traveled from Greece, Italy, and other European nations. In recent years, many people have moved to Australia from Asia in search of better jobs. The largest Asian groups have come from China, India, and Vietnam. Today, about three out of ten Australians were born in another country.

# Speak like an Aussie!

Australians call their mix of English and slang words Strine. Here are some Strine words and their meanings.

| Strine | Meaning |
|--------|---------|
| bonzer | great |
| bush | the countryside |
| g'arn | you're kidding |
| g'day | hello |
| hooroo | good-bye |
| knackered | tired |
| lollies | candy |
| mate | friend |
| Oz | Australia |
| yabber | talk |
| yonks | a long time |

## Did you know?

In 1770, James Cook of the British Navy explored Australia and claimed it for Great Britain. Australia was a British colony until 1901.

## Did you know?

More than 4 million people visit the Sydney Opera House every year. This famous building has a white roof shaped like seashells.

Sydney, Melbourne, Perth, and other large cities are home to most Australians. Shops, theaters, restaurants, and tall office buildings draw people to the city centers. Many Australians live in houses with yards in the nearby **suburbs**. In the Outback, small mining towns and farms lie far apart. Some families live on huge sheep or cattle ranches called **stations**. They might be 100 miles (161 kilometers) or more from the nearest town. Small airplanes are the easiest way to get to a store for food and supplies.

**Where People Live in Australia**

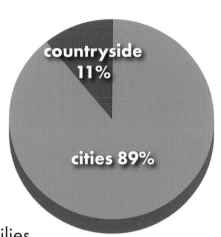

countryside 11%

cities 89%

## fun fact

Australia's largest cattle station covers 9,142 square miles (23,678 square kilometers). That's about the same size as the state of Vermont!

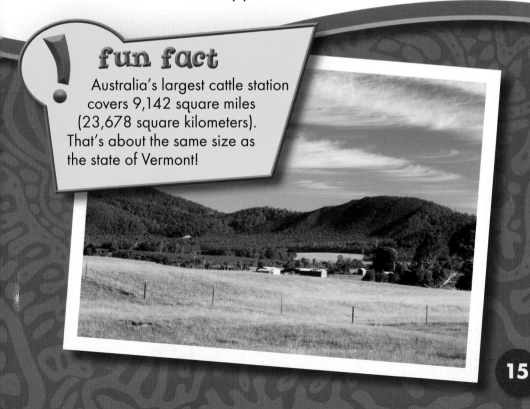

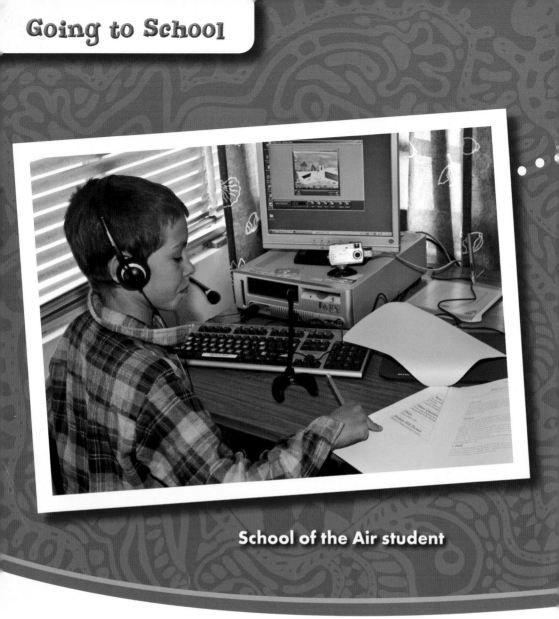

**School of the Air student**

Most Australians start school when they are 5 years old. They study reading, writing, math, and science. Students also learn to use computers and to speak different languages. Kids in cities and towns take classes in school buildings.

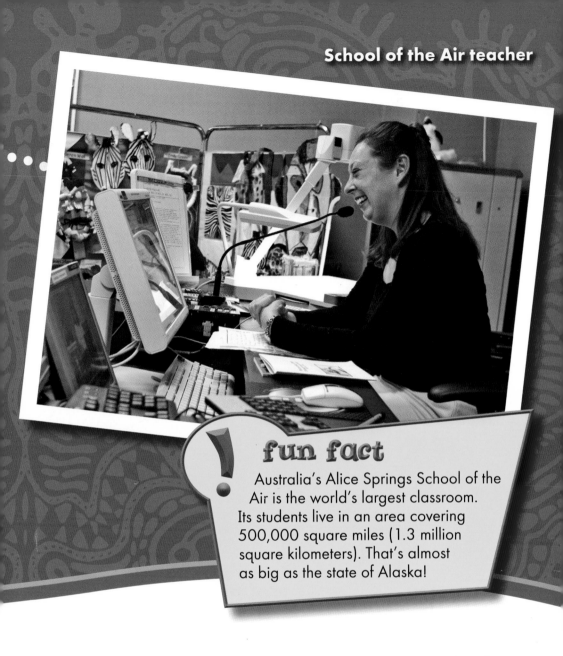

## ! fun fact

Australia's Alice Springs School of the Air is the world's largest classroom. Its students live in an area covering 500,000 square miles (1.3 million square kilometers). That's almost as big as the state of Alaska!

In the Outback, kids live too far apart to go to school together. Instead, they attend Schools of the Air from home. Students watch and listen to their teachers on computers. They e-mail their homework to their teachers.

## Did you know?

Australia has about 90 million sheep! It is the world's largest producer of wool.

## Where People Work in Australia

manufacturing 21%

farming 4%

services 75%

### ! fun fact

Men who work on cattle and sheep stations are called "jackaroos." Women are called "jillaroos." They're all called "roos" for short!

Most Australians hold service jobs. They work in places like hospitals, schools, restaurants, and government offices. Mining is a big business in Australia. Workers dig up coal, diamonds, lead, gold, and many other **minerals**. More than half of Australia is farmland. Farmers grow wheat, sugarcane, grapes, and many other crops. They use most of the land to raise cattle and sheep. Factory workers get minerals and farm products ready to ship all over the world.

# Playing

## fun fact

Australia has more than 10,000 beaches. That's more than any other country in the world!

Australians enjoy many activities in their free time. They go to movies, watch TV, listen to music, and visit friends. Most people live near a beach where they can go swimming, **snorkeling**, and boating. Surfers can catch big waves! On weekends, many Australians go camping or hiking in the **bush**.

Sports are a big part of Australian life. In summer, people play a bat-and-ball sport called cricket. Popular winter sports include soccer and a type of football game called rugby. "Australian rules football," or *footy*, is a rough, fast-moving game. Crowds love to cheer for their favorite *footy* teams.

**Did you know?**

Netball, a game much like basketball, is one of the most popular team sports in Australia.

Many Australians enjoy grilling and eating kangaroo meat. Australia has recently started sending the meat to other countries!

! fun fact
Vegemite is popular in Australia. This salty, bitter spread tops crackers and bread. Many Australians eat it for breakfast.

Australians eat a wide variety of *tucker*. That's what they call food! Meat, potatoes, and vegetables make up many meals. Australians enjoy grilling beef, chicken, and seafood on the *barbie*, or **barbecue**. Immigrants brought many new tastes to Australia. Greek, Italian, Chinese, and Indian dishes are popular. Many Australians enjoy strong black tea called *billy*. They snack on hard cookies called Anzac biscuits. Lamingtons are a sweet treat. These small sponge cakes are dipped in chocolate and coconut.

lamingtons

grilled chicken

Australians come together every year on January 26 for Australia Day. They celebrate the day in 1788 that the first British settlers arrived. There are picnics, parades, and fireworks. Anzac Day is April 25. On this day, Australians honor soldiers who fought and died for their country.

Did you know?
Every year on Australia Day, one person is chosen as the Australian of the Year.

Christmas and New Year's Day are summer holidays. Many people welcome the New Year with barbecues and beach outings. Throughout the year, communities all over Australia hold more than 1,300 fairs and festivals. People gather to enjoy music, dancing, and games.

## Did you know?

Aborigines once hunted with flat, curved sticks called *boomerangs*. They threw *boomerangs* to stun or kill animals. Some *boomerangs* changed direction and returned to the thrower!

**boomerang**

**fun fact**

Aborigines invented a musical instrument called the *didjeridoo* about 1,500 years ago. Many modern musicians still play this long, loud horn made from a hollowed-out tree trunk.

didjeridoo

Aborigines were Australia's first settlers. They have lived in Australia for at least 40,000 years. Long ago, Aborigines were divided into hundreds of groups. Some groups farmed the land. Others walked from place to place to find food and water. Today, only about 2 out of every 100 Australians are Aborigines. Most live modern lives in large cities with other Australians. Some, however, still live in small communities on the lands of their ancestors. Their unique art, storytelling, and music are still an important part of Australia's culture today.

# Fast Facts About Australia

## Australia's Flag

Australia's flag is blue with a small British flag in the upper left corner. A seven-pointed star lies below this flag. Six points of the star stand for Australia's six states. The last point stands for the country's territories. On the right side, five stars make the Southern Cross. This group of stars can be seen in Australia's night sky. Australia has used this flag since 1909.

**Official Name:**   Commonwealth of Australia

**Area:**   2,988,902 square miles (7,741,220 square kilometers); Australia is the 6th largest country in the world.

| | |
|---|---|
| **Capital City:** | Canberra |
| **Important Cities:** | Sydney, Melbourne, Brisbane, Perth, Adelaide, Hobart |
| **Population:** | 21,515,754 (July 2010) |
| **Official Language:** | English |
| **National Holiday:** | Australia Day (January 26) |
| **Religions:** | Christian (63.8%), Unspecified or None (30%), Other (6.2%) |
| **Major Industries:** | farming, manufacturing, mining, services |
| **Natural Resources:** | coal, natural gas, uranium, iron ore, diamonds, lead, gold, opals, timber |
| **Manufactured Products:** | food products, chemicals, machinery, transportation equipment, steel |
| **Farm Products:** | cattle, dairy products, wool, wheat, sugar, fruits, nuts |
| **Unit of Money:** | Australian dollar; the dollar is divided into 100 cents. |

# Glossary

**ancestors**—relatives who lived long ago

**barbecue**—an outdoor grill for cooking food; Australians call a barbecue a *barbie*.

**bush**—Australia's countryside

**continent**—one of the seven main land areas on Earth; the continents are Africa, Antarctica, Asia, Australia, Europe, North America, and South America.

**corals**—small ocean animals whose skeletons make up coral reefs

**dunes**—hills of sand

**equator**—an imaginary line around the center of Earth; the equator divides the planet into a northern half and a southern half.

**eucalyptus**—a strong-smelling evergreen tree that grows in dry regions

**immigrants**—people who leave one country to live in another country

**marsupials**—animals that carry their young in a pouch; a marsupial's pouch is attached to its belly.

**minerals**—elements found in nature; gold, diamonds, and lead are examples of minerals.

**Outback**—the large, inland area of Australia where few people live

**plateaus**—large, flat areas of land that are higher than the surrounding land

**snorkeling**—swimming underwater while breathing through a tube

**stations**—large sheep or cattle ranches

**suburbs**—communities that lie just outside a city; many Australians live in suburbs.

# To Learn More

**AT THE LIBRARY**
Kalman, Bobbie, and Rebecca Sjonger. *Explore Australia and Oceania*. New York, N.Y.: Crabtree Publishing, 2007.

Lumry, Amanda, and Laura Hurwitz. *Riddle of the Reef*. New York, N.Y.: Scholastic, 2009.

Sasek, Miroslav. *This Is Australia*. New York, N.Y.: Universe Publishing, 2009.

**ON THE WEB**
Learning more about Australia is as easy as 1, 2, 3.

1. Go to www.factsurfer.com.

2. Enter "Australia" into the search box.

3. Click the "Surf" button and you will see a list of related Web sites.

With factsurfer.com, finding more information is just a click away.

# Index

The images in this book are reproduced through the courtesy of: Juan Martinez, front cover, pp. 7 (small), 11 (top & middle), 12, 29 (bill); Maisei Raman, front cover (flag), p. 28; Juan Eppardo, pp. 4-5; Ben Heys, pp. 6-7; Debra James, pp. 8-9; Norbert Probst/Photolibrary, p. 9 (small); J & C Sohns/Photolibrary, pp. 10-11; Rafael Ramirez Lee, p. 11 (bottom); Jose Fuste Raga/Photolibrary, p. 14; Ashley Whitworth/ Alamy, p. 15; Bill Bachman/Alamy, pp. 16, 17; John White Photos/Getty Images, p. 18; R. Ian Lloyd/ Masterfile, p. 19 (left); Monty Rakusen/Photolibrary, p. 19 (right); David Morgan/Alamy, p. 20; Christopher Lee/Stringer/Getty Images, p. 21; FoodCollection/Photolibrary, p. 22; Robyn Mackenzie, pp. 23 (top), 29 (coin); Elena Elisseeva, p. 23 (bottom); Andrew Watson/Photolibrary, pp. 24-25; Dallas and John Heaton/Alamy, p. 26; David Hill/Alamy, p. 27.